D1245286

DON'T BE THAT KID!™
AT SCHOOL

RESOURCE GUIDE

Lois McGuire

TELEMACHUS PRESS

DON'T BE THAT KID!™ AT SCHOOL RESOURCE GUIDE

Don't Be That Kid!™ is a Trademark of Lois McGuire

Cover and interior art by Jorge Pacheco

Chart Paper ©Copyright Chaoss | Dreamstime.com_2038743

Visit the author website: www.dontbethatkid.net

ISBN# 978-1-942899-95-2 (Paperback)

Library of Congress Control Number: 2016953462

Published by: Telemachus Press, LLC
Visit our website: http://www.telemachuspress.com

Printed in the United States of America
10 9 8 7 6 5 4 3 2 1

Version: 2016.10.20

Table of Contents

Establishing Expectations 1

Extension Activities 13

 Learning From Elders 15

 Learning Bus Safety 19

 Learning To Respect Others' Space 23

 Learning To Be Honest 26

 Learning To Be Organized 29

 Learning To Include Others 32

 Learning To Be Considerate 35

 Learning To Respect Others' Property 38

 Learning To Be Responsible 41

 Learning To Solve Problems 44

 Learning To Be Kind 47

 Learning To Be Respectful 50

 Learning To Be Positive 53

 Learning To Make Good Choices 56

 Learning To Complete Tasks 59

 Learning Self-Reflection 62

Resources - May be reproduced 65

 Kid Profile 67

 Don't Be That KID! Pledge 69

 Family Crest 71

About the Author 73

About the Illustrator 74

DON'T BE THAT KID!™
AT SCHOOL

RESOURCE GUIDE

GETTING STARTED

Welcome to the Don't Be That KID! At School Resource Guide! The Guide was developed to assist you to establish expectations for classroom and school behaviors that can be expanded to any setting.

After reading the book to the class, please don't put it on a shelf! Keep Don't Be That KID! At School alive in your classroom as a mentor text. Use the Don't Be That KID! At School extension activities to reinforce classroom and school behaviors, student expectations and character education standards throughout the year. Please note that all of the activities are adaptable to any grade level and students' abilities. The teacher may determine the amount of time spent on each activity depending on student or class needs.

Lois McGuire

ESTABLISHING EXPECTATIONS

Grades K – 1

Day 1:

After reading Don't Be That KID! At School, discuss the last page and ask the students to tell you why the KID is now wearing a bright shirt. Ask questions, such as, "What will the KID have to do to change his behavior?" and "Why do we need classroom and school rules?" Chart student responses and post in the classroom as a reference for future lessons or discussions. See a sample chart below:

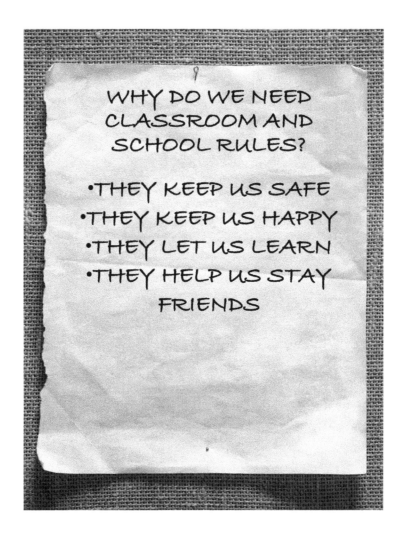

You may want to add pictures to your chart so non-readers can independently understand the chart.

Say to the class, "Let's think of some rules that will help us to learn this year." As students tell you some rules, write them down on chart paper. They should be simple and positive, such as, "Raise my hand before I speak" and "Keep my hands to myself." Limit the number of rules at this grade level. Once complete, display the rules chart in a prominent location in the classroom. A sample chart is below:

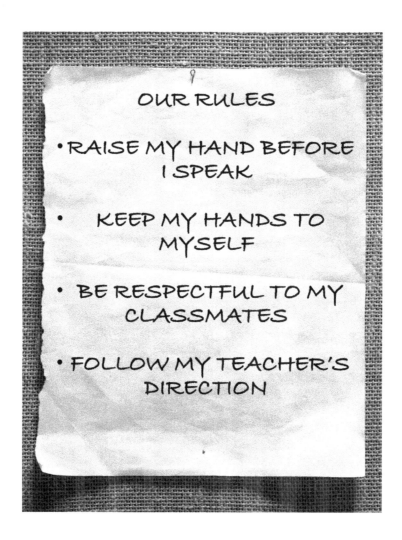

Distribute the KID Profile at the back of the Resource Guide. Ask the students to color him now that he is going to be following the rules. Ask students to tell their KID one behavior goal they will set for themselves for the beginning of the school year. Hang the KIDs around the classroom as a reminder of these goals.

Day 2:

Laminate the rules chart and hang it in the classroom. Replicate the classroom chart and create mini-charts to distribute to students to place in their folders. Discuss possible rewards for following the rules and possible consequences for not following the rules. Students complete the Don't Be That KID! Pledge which may be found in the back of the Resource Guide.

Notes

Grades 2 – 3

Day 1:

After reading Don't Be That KID! At School, discuss the significance of the KID now wearing a bright shirt. Have a classroom discussion regarding the fact that students are in control of their own behavior and the importance of being able to change behavior to comply with rules and expectations. Ask students to turn and talk to their partners about why we need classroom and school rules. Create a chart with a list of ten "BE's". A sample chart is below:

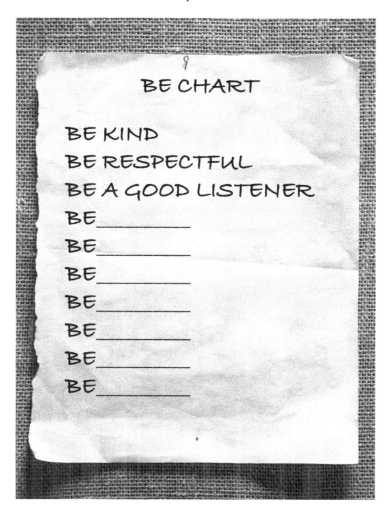

After completing the list, extend it as a group discussion to compile your classroom rules on chart paper. It may look like this:

BE KIND to each other every day.

BE RESPECTFUL of everyone's ideas.

BE A GOOD LISTENER when someone else is speaking.

The final result should be simple but well defined. Display the BE chart in a prominent place in the classroom.

Day 2:

Laminate the BE chart and hang it in the classroom. Replicate the BE chart and create mini-charts to distribute to students to place in their folders. Discuss the importance of following these class created rules. Discuss what could happen to the learning environment if the rules aren't followed by each student. Discuss possible rewards if the rules are followed as well as possible consequences if the rules are not followed. The rewards and consequences should come from the students with teacher guidance. The teacher should guide students to select rewards and consequences that can easily be enforced. Chart rewards and consequences. A sample chart is below:

REWARDS: WHEN THE ENTIRE CLASS EARNS 10 BE GOOD POINTS

- SHOW AND TELL or

- CLASS PARTY or

- PAJAMA DAY

CONSEQUENCES: WHEN A STUDENT DOESN'T FOLLOW A CLASS RULE

- 1ST BROKEN BE: WARNING

- 2ND BROKEN BE: MISS 10 MINUTES OF RECESS

- 3RD BROKEN BE: MISS FULL RECESS

- 4TH BROKEN BE: PHONE CALL HOME

The teacher may also make this chart into mini-charts and place them in the students' folders on Day 3. Ask each student to set a behavior goal for the first month of school and record their personal goal on their mini-chart. Students complete the Don't Be That KID! Pledge.

Notes

Grades 4 -5

Day 1:

After reading Don't Be That KID! At School, have the students brainstorm and record the ways in which each negative KID behavior on each page can be changed into a positive behavior. Two examples are:

pp. 12 & 13: Include others when playing any game or sport.

pp. 14 & 15: Keep your personal area neat.

Engage students in a classroom discussion to share their newly created lists of positive behaviors. From their lists, categorize the behaviors into school expectations (hallway, recess, cafeteria, etc.) and classroom behaviors for the general classroom as well as for special subject area classrooms. Use this list to develop a chart of classroom and school expectations. Have the students copy the chart into their folders or notebooks. Explain that this is a "rough draft". Ask them to review these expectations tonight and make any additions they think important. In addition, ask the students to begin to think about possible rewards if expectations are met and possible consequences if expectations are not followed.

Day 2:

Review the classroom and school expectations, adding and deleting content in response to students' ideas. Explain that in life, there are consequences to every decision a person makes and students in the classroom will also experience consequences for their actions. Consequences can be positive (rewards) when students abide by the rules or negative (penalties) when students break the rules. Complete a chart of both positive and negative consequences that coordinate with the expectations. Sample charts are on pp. 9 - 11:

CLASSROOM EXPECTATIONS

- ACTIVELY LISTEN WHILE OTHERS ARE SPEAKING

- KEEP YOUR DESK NEAT AND ORGANIZED

- USE YOUR BEST EFFORT IN ALL ASSIGNMENTS

SCHOOL EXPECTATIONS

- WALK CALMLY AND QUIETLY IN HALLWAYS

- BE RESPECTFUL TO STUDENTS AND TEACHERS

- INCLUDE ALL STUDENTS AND MAKE EVERYONE FEEL WELCOME

REWARDS: WHEN A STUDENT EXCEEDS EXPECTATIONS

- MENTOR PERIOD – STUDENT CAN BE AIDE IN A FIRST GRADE CLASS or

- STUDENT CAN TEACH A CLASS LESSON or

- STUDENT CAN HELP PLAN A CLASS TRIP

REWARDS: WHEN THE CLASS EXCEEDS EXPECTATIONS

- TEACHER EATS IN CAFETERIA WITH STUDENTS or

- CRAZY HAT/HAIR DAY or

- CLASS PARTY

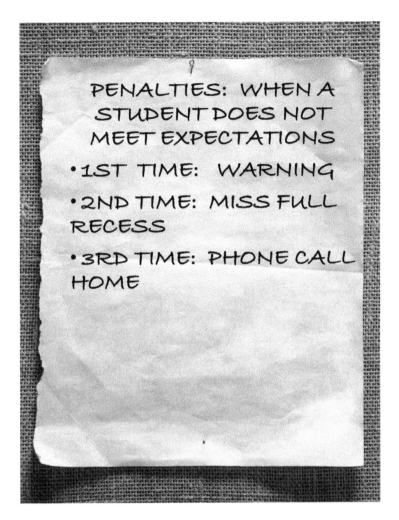

The students will copy the final expectations and coordinating consequences in their folders or notebooks and set a behavior goal for the first month of school. They will also complete the Don't Be That KID! Pledge.

Notes

DON'T BE THAT KID!™
AT SCHOOL

EXTENSION ACTIVITIES

LEARNING FROM ELDERS

Reference Pages 2 & 3

Grades K - 1

Ask the class, "How many of you brush your own teeth?" "Who taught you to do that?" "How many of you know how to ride a bike?" "Who taught you to do that?" Say, "Just like the grownups in our lives teach us how to do things, they also teach us important life lessons." Tell the students a personal story about a life lesson you learned from an elder. The following is an example:

> *My grandparents owned a store that sold lamps and gift items. When I was a little girl, I would spend every Saturday at their store. Every person who came into the store was treated with respect and kindness whether or not they purchased anything. My grandmother and grandfather taught me that you always speak to a person politely and try to assist them if you can. Whether they buy something or not, always say "thank you". I learned how to treat people respectfully by watching my grandparents wait on customers.*

Say to the class, "I want you to think of some good advice a grandparent or parent has given you." List the responses on chart paper and when it's completed, read each one. As you read over the list, ask the students to put their thumbs up if they think it is good advice. Discuss the importance of learning from older, more experienced family members. Ask students to draw a picture of their family. If students can write, have them label the people in their picture. The teacher may assist students by listing possible family members on the board or on a chart (Mom, Dad, Sister, Brother, Grandmother, Uncle, Dog, Cat, etc.). Students who know how to write can write the given advice under their family drawing. The teacher can script the advice students were given on each non-writer's drawing. Some students may need a sentence starter statement such as: I should always _____. I learned _____. My _____gave me the advice to _____. One of my family lessons is _____.

Notes

Grades 2 -3

Write on the board: "How can we learn from past experiences or mistakes?" Tell the students a personal story about a mistake you made in the past and the lesson you learned. Ask the students to write down something that they did (positive or negative) and what they learned from it. Have students volunteer to read what they wrote to the class. Discuss the importance of listening and learning from elders and family members. Discuss family crests and show an example of your family crest. Distribute the blank Family Crest found in the back of the Resource Guide to each student and ask them to design it making sure they include the values they have learned from their family members.

Notes

Grades 4 – 5

Share a personal story about a time you learned from an experience. Discuss how we can learn from all of our experiences. Stress the importance of listening and leaning from more- experienced family members and elders. Assign the students the task of interviewing a parent or grandparent. Students will ask their parent or grandparent to share a life experience and the lesson they learned from it. The students will write a paragraph summarizing what they were told in the interview. They will write a second paragraph explaining what they learned from their elder by listening about their experience. Students will share their paragraphs with the class.

Notes

LEARNING BUS SAFETY

Reference Pages 4 & 5

National Bus Safety Week is usually held the third week in October. The following list of rules has been compiled from various bus safety councils:

At the Bus Stop:

- Always walk, not run, to the bus stop.
- Walk on the sidewalk. If there is no sidewalk, walk on the left facing traffic.
- Be at the bus stop at least 5 minutes before the bus is scheduled to arrive.
- Wait in a safe place away from the road. Reserve running or playing for the playground.
- Only speak to people you know at the bus stop and never get into a car with a stranger.
- Watch for the red flashing lights and the stop sign to be extended when the bus arrives.
- Cross the street only when all traffic has stopped. Look left, right and left again before crossing.
- Wait until the bus has stopped and the door opens before approaching the bus.
- Use the handrail when boarding.

On the Bus:

- Walk directly to a seat. Remain seated and facing forward for the entire ride.
- Talk quietly so the driver will not be distracted.

- If you need to speak to the driver, wait for the bus to stop, raise your hand, and call the driver by name.
- Keep all items inside the bus; never throw things on the bus or out the window.
- Keep your head, arms and hands inside the bus at all times and away from the windows.
- Keep aisles clear of books and bags.
- Never play with the emergency exits.
- Wait for the bus to stop completely before getting up from your seat.

Getting Off the Bus:

- Walk towards the exit.
- Use the handrail when exiting.
- Walk away from the door and keep away from the bus' wheels.
- Wait for a signal from the bus driver before crossing the street. Look left, right, then left again. Be alert for moving cars.
- If you leave something on the bus, do not return to get it. The driver may not know you are on the bus and could move the bus.
- Only get off the bus at your designated stop unless you have a note from a parent.
- If you drop something near the bus, tell the bus driver. Do not go near the wheels.
- Go straight home so an adult will know where you are.

Grades K - 1

Ask one of the school bus drivers to come to the class to speak to the students about student bus safety and how students can help bus drivers keep the bus a safe and happy place for children. After the presentation, ask the students what they learned and record their responses on chart paper. Write a group "thank you" note to the bus driver. Include lessons learned in the note.

Notes

Grades 2 - 3

Discuss the safety rules with the class. Initiate a grade level poster contest depicting proper bus safety. Hang the posters throughout the school during Bus Safety Week.

Notes

Grades 4 - 5

Students work in pairs. Each pair chooses one safety rule and creates a book page describing and illustrating the rule. The class creates a book that they then can read to students in grades K – 3. Once shared with younger students, 4th and 5th graders donate their completed books to primary grade classrooms.

Notes

LEARNING TO RESPECT OTHERS' SPACE

Reference Pages 6 & 7

Grades K - 1

Play "Simon Says" with the class. Afterwards, discuss the parts of the body and the importance of respecting everyone's "space" and keeping hands and feet where they belong. Explain that respecting others' space also includes respecting their desks, cubbies and lockers. Practice walking on line in the hall, getting water from the water fountain, going to cubbies and/or lockers at the end of the day. Refer back to the classroom rules posted since the beginning of the school year. Ask the class to provide additional rules that pertain to respecting others' body space and area space and add them to the rules chart. Some examples of being aware of body and area space are: in the gym, in the school yard, at home with brothers and sisters, at restaurants, etc. Present students with some personal space scenarios and have them work in pairs to act out these personal space problems and solutions. Share mini-skits with the class.

Notes

Grades 2 - 3

Discuss the concept of everyone being entitled to their own "space". Explain that your personal "space" is like an invisible shield or a bubble surrounding you. Distribute paper with a list of positive and negative touching. Some examples are: (1) giving a "high- five" slap; (2) shoving someone ahead of you on line; (3) tripping someone; (4) shaking hands; (5) giving a pat on the back; (6) pulling hair; (7) giving a hug; (8) poking someone with a pencil; (9) elbowing someone; (10) holding hands. Ask the students to categorize each item in either a positive or negative column using a t chart. Have the students write a paragraph about the importance of respecting everyone's individual "space" and what steps they can take to follow safe space rules.

Notes

Grades 4 - 5

Explain that personal "space" refers to the physical distance between people in social, family, work and school situations. Afterwards, students will work in pairs to complete rules of etiquette regarding respecting someone's personal "space". Some examples are: (1) only touch those you know who welcome the touch; (2) respect others' privacy; never go through someone else's belongings; (3) take your proper place in line; don't cut in line; (4) find your own seat; don't take another person's seat; (5) reserve cell phone use to quiet conversations. Have the students share their rules with the class. Have the students continue to work in pairs to create examples of what a person can do if his personal "space" is invaded, such as (1) lean away; (2) take a step back; (3) tell the person you are uncomfortable; (4) inform an adult. Students can act out these personal space dilemmas and solutions in front of the class.

Notes

LEARNING TO BE HONEST

Reference Pages 8 & 9

Grades K – 1

Explain that cheating on a test is dishonest. Have a classroom discussion centering on why the KID felt he had to cheat (examples include: he didn't study, he wants to get the highest grade possible, he doesn't think it is wrong). Extend the discussion to how the girl he is cheating from might feel (examples include: she is afraid the teacher will think she is cheating too, she is angry at the KID). Ask, "What are some things you can do if someone is cheating from you?" (examples include: speak to them after the test, cover your paper, tell an adult). Ask the students to tell other examples of not being honest (examples include: taking something that doesn't belong to you, not telling the truth). Write each response on the board or chart paper. Distribute paper titled "LEARNING ABOUT HONESTY" with two columns. One column is labeled "Not Honest", the other " Honest". Students write the list from the board or chart paper in the first column and then write a sentence explaining how to change the dishonest behavior to honest behavior in the second column. An example is below:

LEARNING ABOUT HONESTY

Not Honest	Honest
Taking something that isn't yours	Asking someone to borrow something

Notes

Grades 2 – 3

Google quotes on honesty and post quotes on chart paper and hang the charts around the classroom. Conduct a "write around". Give students 15 minutes to walk around the room and write their thoughts concerning the quotes on each chart. Students should write their ideas right onto the chart paper so their classmates can read and respond to their ideas as well as to the quotes. After time is up, ask students to once again walk around the room, read the charts and think about the quotes and student written responses. Ask students to return to their desks, choose one quote, and record it and some of their reflections as well as their classmates' reflections. For homework, the students write a paragraph on what the quote means to them and another paragraph on who the author is. Two examples are:

"Our greatest weakness lies in giving up. The most certain way to succeed is always to try just one more time." - Thomas A. Edison

"To know what is right and not do it is the worse cowardice." – Confucius

Notes

Grades 4 – 5

Write the Benjamin Franklin quote, "Honesty Is the Best Policy." on the board. Discuss the basic tenets of honesty with the class. Then write underneath the quote: "Is honesty always the best policy?" Students will work in pairs to debate both sides of the question. Once pairs engage in debate time, the "pro honesty" and "con honesty" teams will quorum and prepare a presentation of the points of view to the class. After each makes their presentations, the class will reach consensus on an honesty thesis.

Notes

LEARNING TO BE ORGANIZED

Reference Pages 10 & 11

Grades K – 1

Work with the students to create a list of tasks that are needed each day to assure the classroom runs smoothly. Chart ideas. Some examples are: pencil monitor, trash monitor, weather announcer, morning message announcer, pet helper. Discuss the importance of organization to accomplish each task. Write each job (or paste a picture) on a bulletin board. List the step by step tasks needed to be successful under each job. Select different students each week to accomplish the tasks.

Notes

Grades 2 – 3

Explain that sometimes being organized requires setting goals. Distribute paper with the following three questions for students to answer: "What are your top 3 goals for the year?"; "What will you have to do to achieve each one?"; "How will you know if you achieved them?" Distribute an action plan template. Model how to create an action plan. Ask students to create plans for their 3 goals.

Notes

Grades 4 – 5

Discuss that being organized requires a vision of what you want to accomplish. Review the mission statement of your school. Create a classroom mission statement. Collect pictures from magazines and spread them out around the classroom. Ask students to walk around the room and select a picture that they think represents their personal goals and personal mission. Ask students to write a reflection of how the picture reflects their personal mission. Students may also design a logo to represent their mission.

Notes

LEARNING TO INCLUDE OTHERS

Reference Pages 12 & 13

Grades K – 1

Students make happy and sad face squares. Distribute paper titled: "HOW WOULD YOU FEEL IF…". List 10 possible scenarios and read each one to students who paste either a happy or sad face next to it. Some examples are: (1) You were not invited to a party; (2) No one sat next to you in cafeteria; (3) You were asked to play a game; (4) You didn't receive any Valentine's Day cards; (5) Someone shared their toy with you.

Notes

Grades 2 – 3

Develop classroom interview questions. Students work in pairs and interview one another. Distribute a Venn diagram with each student's name on each side. The students complete the Venn diagram, writing in their differences on the two ends and similarities in the center. Afterwards, students introduce the person they interviewed to the class and share commonalities and differences with the class.

Notes

Grades 4 – 5

Students work in groups of 6 and create a scene that depicts ways to include students in different scenarios. Some examples are: (1) a new student in school; (2) a student who doesn't know how to play a game; (3) a shy student; (4) a student who doesn't speak English well; (5) a student from another culture; (6) a student picked last to be on a team. They write a script and then act out their scene to the class. Students may also share these scenes with students in other grade levels.

Notes

LEARNING TO BE CONSIDERATE

Reference Pages 14 & 15

Grades K – 1

Explain to the class that being considerate is thinking of others. Ask the class what actions make the KID in the book inconsiderate. Record the list on chart paper (examples include: messy desk, leaning back, paper airplane, not paying attention, etc.). Ask the class to tell you some considerate things they have done. Some examples are: dried the dishes, played with sister, put toys away. Write the list on another piece of chart paper. Distribute paper titled "BEING CONSIDERATE". Have students choose one of the considerate gestures already listed on the chart paper or add one of their own. Students then draw a picture illustrating the considerate action. Students who are writers may choose to label their picture or write sentences to describe their considerate action. Teachers may hang the projects around the classroom.

Notes

Grades 2 – 3

Discuss what it means to be considerate of others. Distribute magazines to each student or have them research images on the Internet. Have them cut out a picture of someone being considerate and write a paragraph underneath explaining why they selected that picture to depict consideration.

Notes

Grades 4 – 5

Discuss what it means to be considerate of others. Ask the class, "What can you learn from being considerate?" Discuss fables and the role of a moral. Read a fable with a moral concerning consideration to the class. Work with the school librarian to gather fables from various countries and have available in the classroom for students to use as mentor texts. Have the students work in pairs to write and illustrate their own fable about being considerate. The students will share their fables with the class.

Notes

LEARNING TO RESPECT OTHERS' PROPERTY

Reference Pages 16 & 17

Earth Day is usually held in April.

Grades K – 1

Discuss the importance of Earth Day and having each individual take care of his/her things. Distribute paper and ask students to draw a picture of their favorite possession. Afterwards, students work in pairs and share their drawings and discuss the answers to the following questions: (1) Why is the item your prized possession? (2) How do you take care of your prized possession? The pairs then introduce their partners to the entire class and share the information they learned about the prized possession with the class. Extend the activity by discussing respecting other people's property. Distribute paper titled: "HOW WOULD YOU FEEL IF…" List questions such as: (1) Someone took your sweater? (2) Someone broke your computer? (3) Someone threw dirty clothes into your bedroom? Students may answer each question either through partner talk or independently, in writing.

Notes

Grades 2 – 3

Begin the lesson by saying, "Let's talk today about respecting the things we own and respecting other people's property." Discuss Earth Day and then write on the board: REDUCE REUSE RECYCLE. Students work in pairs to list what they can do in each category. Some examples are: REDUCE the number of sheets of paper towels I use each day; REUSE a plastic container by washing out its contents; RECYCLE all bottles. Students share what they wrote with the class.

Notes

Grades 4 – 5

Discuss Earth Day with the class. Write the following question on the board: What are some issues regarding disrespecting property in (1) Our School; (2) Your Home; (3) Your Neighborhood; (4) Our Community. Students work in groups of three and select one issue in each area. They state the issue, develop a plan to alleviate the problem and explain how they will evaluate its success. Each group presents to the class.

Notes

LEARNING TO BE RESPONSIBLE

Reference Pages 18 & 19

Grades K – 1

Ask the students to tell you some of their responsibilities. Some examples are: picking up toys, choosing what to wear, completing homework, putting clothes in the hamper, drying dishes, brushing teeth, etc. List their responses on chart paper or on the board. Afterwards have each student categorize the responsibilities into Morning Responsibilities, Afternoon Responsibilities, Night Time Responsibilities. Make the point that some of their responsibilities occur more than just once a day.

Notes

Grades 2 – 3

Distribute paper with three columns: Home Responsibilities, School Responsibilities, Personal Responsibilities. Ask students to list 5 responsibilities under each one. An example is below:

<u>Home Responsibilities</u>   <u>School Responsibilities</u>   <u>Personal Responsibilities</u>

Clean my room   Do my homework   Brush my teeth

Afterwards, each student makes an "I AM RESPONSIBLE" mobile. Teachers may hang mobiles throughout the classroom.

Notes

Grades 4 – 5

Explain to the class that learning to be responsible means being accountable for your actions. Ask the students to write a minimum of two paragraphs on the topic: "How Can I Improve Myself?" The teacher will model how to use these paragraphs to create goals. Afterwards, the teacher will model how to turn goals into action plans. Students will set their own goals and create their own action plans.

Notes

LEARNING TO SOLVE PROBLEMS

Reference Pages 20 & 21

Grades K – 1

Discuss the fact that fighting never solves problems and there are good ways that problems can be solved. For example, understanding your feelings and being able to express your feelings to a friend or an adult could help you solve a problem. Have the class make a list of feelings (happy, sad, angry, upset, confused, hurt, etc.) and list them on chart paper. Afterwards, write each feeling on a sheet of paper and distribute it to the students. Have them draw an appropriate face to match each one. Afterwards, students role-play how to act when they have different feelings.

Notes

Grades 2 – 3

Discuss the importance of learning self-control and the fact that students have control over their own words and actions. Ask students to list ways that they can solve problems to prevent improper behaviors like being mean, fighting and name-calling. Afterwards, students will create and illustrate a Problem Solving Deck of 10 Cards. Some examples are: (1) Ask for Help; (2) Apologize; (3) Walk Away; (4) Count to 10; (5) Ask Them to Stop; (6) Ignore Them. Teachers can remind students to use the cards as reminders and problem solving tools as behaviors and concerns surface in the future.

Notes

Grades 4 – 5

Discuss the importance of being able to express yourself in order to solve problems and prevent arguments and fighting. Introduce the concept of "I-Messages". Explain that sometimes we feel upset by things someone else has done and we should be able to discuss it with that person. We need to tell them how we feel, what upset us and what we want to see happen. Using "I-Messages" allows us to talk about an issue rather than calling people names or fighting with them. Distribute a sheet of paper with the "I-Message" formula written on it:

I feel _____(insert feeling word) when you _____(what caused the feeling) and I would like_____(what you want to happen instead)

Give a specific example, such as: I feel <u>angry</u> when you <u>take my video game</u> and would like <u>you to ask to borrow it</u>.

Practice using "I-Messages". Afterwards, give students scenarios and ask them to complete the "I-Message" to resolve each situation.

Notes

LEARNING TO BE KIND

Reference Pages 22 & 23

Random Acts of Kindness Month is usually held in February.

Grades K – 1

Explain that learning to listen to others is respectful and kind. It shows someone that you care about them. Read "The Giving Tree" by Shel Silverstein. Have a class discussion regarding what the book means to them. Questions may include: "Was the boy a good listener?" "Was the tree a good listener?" "Was the boy kind?" "Was the tree kind?" Discuss acts of kindness and make a short list on chart paper. Create a Tree of Kindness for Random Acts of Kindness Month. When a student does something kind, place his/her name on the tree and write the act of kindness under it.

Notes

Grades 2 – 3

Discuss the importance of treating everyone with respect and kindness. Ask the class, "How does it feel to receive a compliment?" "How does it feel to receive a 'put down'?" The students will move from seat to seat and share one compliment with each of their classmates until every student has heard from each student in the class. Afterwards, the students write a paragraph explaining how the activity made them feel. They will then set a kindness goal. The teacher could provide prompts such as: It makes me feel good when _____ so I will _____ for others. In the month of February, my goal is to _____ to make others feel good.

Notes

Grades 4 – 5

Discuss the importance of treating everyone with respect and kindness. Expand it to talk about being able to express how you feel about someone verbally or in writing. As a group, make a list of 25 random acts of kindness (mowing your neighbor's lawn, helping a toddler climb stairs, etc.). Ask each student to keep a journal of each act of kindness they do for the month of February. At the end of the month, have students reflect on how these random acts of kindness made others feel as well as how it made them feel. The students may share their journals and reflections with the class.

Notes

LEARNING TO BE RESPECTFUL

Reference Pages 24 & 25

Grades K – 1

Explain the importance of learning to respect yourself and others. Discuss what the KID in the book is doing that is disrespectful. Distribute paper divided into quarters. Label the title: "SHOWING RESPECT". Write in box 1: AT HOME; BOX 2: AT SCHOOL; BOX 3: AT PLAY; BOX 4: IN THE NEIGBORHOOD. Have students draw a picture of how they show respect in each box. Students who are writers may label their pictures or write sentences under each picture.

Notes

Grades 2 – 3

Distribute paper divided into quarters. Label the title: "A RESPECTFUL PERSON." Write in box 1: IS; box 2: DOES; box 3: SAYS; box 4: IS NOT. Students list actions under each box, such as: IS (Kind, Honest, Helpful, Friendly); DOES (Helps Others, Shares, Includes Others); SAYS (Please, Thank You, I'm Sorry, Let Me Help); IS NOT (Rude, Mean, Impatient, Fresh). Students share their lists. The teacher may create a class bulletin board using these artifacts.

Notes

Grades 4 – 5

Play Aretha Franklin's song "RESPECT". Discuss the importance of learning to respect yourself and others. Ask the class to give specific examples of respectful and disrespectful behaviors. Work with the school music teacher to introduce the class to different music genres. Have the students work in groups of 4 to write a song, cheer or rap about respect. Students may perform their creations for the class and possibly for other classes.

Notes

LEARNING TO BE POSITIVE

Reference Pages 26 & 27

Grades K – 1

Draw a happy face and a sad face on the board. Explain that the happy face is positive; the sad face negative. Ask the students to tell about times they acted positive and negative. Write BEING POSITIVE on chart paper. On one side write LOOKS LIKE; on the other side SOUNDS LIKE. Students brainstorm what being positive looks like and sounds like. The teacher lists their responses on each side of the chart. Some examples for LOOKS LIKE are: Participating, Waiting my turn, Sharing, Careful listening, Using my best effort, Not giving up, Trying new things. Examples for SOUNDS LIKE are: Excuse me, Please, Thank you, No thank you, Let me help, I can do it, Let's work together.

Notes

Grades 2 – 3

Fill two jars halfway with jellybeans. Explain that some people would say the jars are half -empty; others would say they are half-full. Ask them which answer sounds positive; which sounds negative. Explain that being positive means feeling good about yourself and being involved with friends and family. Explain that you can learn to approach things in a positive rather than negative manner. Ask each student to create a greeting card that shows a positive outlook. Students may share their cards with the class and eat the jellybeans!

Notes

Grades 4 – 5

Explain that sometimes it isn't easy to remain positive when negative things happen to you but it's important to work hard at it. Have the class tell you 10 things that have happened to them that made it difficult to remain positive. Write them on the board. Some examples are: (1) lost a basketball game; (2) favorite pet died; (3) failed a test; (4) argued with a friend. Have the class write examples of turning these negatives into positives. Do the first one together: Lost a basketball game: (1) the team played well but lost in final seconds; (2) I personally played well; (3) we were good sports. Students may share their answers with the class.

Notes

LEARNING TO MAKE GOOD CHOICES

Reference Page 28 & 29

Grades K – 1

Explain to the class that every day we make lots of choices. Discuss some choices they made that day, such as: what they ate for breakfast; what they are wearing; where they sat on the bus. Discuss the importance of thinking about a choice before we decide. Distribute paper titled "MAKING CHOICES" with two columns. One column is labeled "Bad Choices"; the other column "Good Choices". Make a list of bad choices on the left and students write a corresponding good choice on the right. An example is below:

MAKING CHOICES

BAD CHOICES	BECOME GOOD CHOICES
Hitting	Walking away
Cheating	Studying
Leaving clothes on the floor	Hanging clothes in the closet
Frowning	Smiling

Notes

Grades 2 – 3

Ask the students to think of a choice they had to make. An example might be a time when they were invited to two birthday parties on the same day. Have the class brainstorm solutions to the presented dilemma. An example is: Go to both and stay for shorter times at each. Ask the class to write answers to the following questions written on the board: (1) What was a choice you had to make? (2) What were some of the options you considered? (3) What did you choose to do? (4) Why did you make that choice? (5) What was the result?

Notes

Grades 4 – 5

Introduce the concept of having a Class Meeting once each month. Explain that these meetings would present an opportunity for the class to work out classroom or school-related issues as they arise and help the students in solving problems rather than relying on the teacher to solve them. The teacher should lead the first few meetings and determine when the students are ready to select a fellow student to lead it. Stress that an issue may be a problem (such as a student to student argument) or a topic of interest (such as discussing field trip possibilities). The class should generate meeting rules and the teacher should chart them. Examples may include the following list:

1. Students submit an issue for discussion prior to the meeting.
2. The number of issues to be discussed each meeting will be limited depending on the time needed for each issue.
3. The student who submitted the issue will describe the issue.
4. Students give their thoughts and ideas about the topic.
5. Students provide proposals for a solution to the topic.
6. A solution and timeline is agreed upon.
7. The minutes of the meeting are written by a student and placed in a Class Meeting Log.

Notes

LEARNING TO COMPLETE TASKS

Reference Pages 30 & 31

Grades K – 1

Review the daily class schedule with the students. Explain that each activity is completed within a timeframe and it is important to learn to finish tasks in a timely manner. Have the class give examples of tasks they have to complete and write them on the board (examples include: homework, tests, putting toys away, etc.). Play "Beat the Clock" with the class by giving students a specific time to complete a task, such as sharpening three pencils; putting crayons back in their boxes; putting books in cubbies. Afterwards, discuss the importance of determining how long something may take to complete so you will have enough time. The teacher may ask the students to set time goals for some of their work. For example: It will take _____minutes for me to complete my math page; it will take _____minutes for me to read my book; it will take _____minutes for me to write to the marked line on my page.

Notes

Grades 2 – 3

Write the word PROCRASTINATE on the board. Ask the class what it means. Write the definition on the board. Discuss why people procrastinate (examples include: the task is too difficult; don't enjoy the activity; don't think it's a priority, feeling lazy; etc.). Write the question: "What can happen if you procrastinate?" on the board and have a classroom discussion (examples include: don't finish your schoolwork; late for school; late for a movie; miss an opportunity). Have the students write two paragraphs about a time they procrastinated, what happened as a result, and what they learned from the experience.

Notes

Grades 4 – 5

Explain the importance of completing tasks in a timely manner. Discuss the reasons why people procrastinate and what can result. Ask the class to make a TO DO LIST of what they want to accomplish this week. Include a timeline to accomplish each task. Some examples are:

TO DO LIST

ACTIVITY	TIME NEEDED	COMPLETION DATE
Clean My Room	2 Hours	Saturday
Finish Science Project	3 Hours	Sunday
Play Basketball	3 Hours	Wednesday
Complete Homework	2 Hours	Each Night
Give Dog a Bath	1 Hour	Friday

Notes

LEARNING SELF-REFLECTION

Reference Pages 32 & 33

Grades K – 1

Explain that the KID in the book is looking in the mirror and seeing his reflection. Throughout the book he is misbehaving but now he is "reflecting" on what he has done and wants to change. Display a chart of all the lessons learned from the book and review each lesson learned: Learning from Elders; Learning Safety; Respecting Others' Space; Learning Honesty; Including Others; Being Considerate; Respecting Property; Being Responsible; Solving Problems; Being Kind; Being Respectful; Being Positive; Making Good Choices; Completing Tasks; and Learning About Ourselves. Explain that these are all excellent qualities and that if students work hard they can achieve each one. Distribute paper and ask the class to pretend they are looking in the mirror. Ask students to draw a self-portrait and list at least 3 positive qualities they already see in themselves. Teachers may hang the portraits in the classroom to remind students of their positive qualities.

Notes

Grades 2 – 3

Discuss that the KID is looking in the mirror and seeing his reflection. Have a class discussion about how we see ourselves and how others may see us. Ask the question: "Is it possible that they are not the same?" List the lessons learned from the book (see Grades K – 1 on page 62) and reiterate what each one means and how we can achieve them. Stress that each person is an individual and unique in his/her own way. Distribute the KID in the back of the Resource Guide. Students will create a unique KID at home by decorating it with words and images that represent their own unique, positive qualities. Students can use any materials they wish and the KID can look any way each student wants. However, the KID must incorporate at least 5 qualities about themselves. The teacher may hang the KIDS around the classroom.

Notes

Grades 4 – 5

Show a clip from the Snow White video in which the witch holds up a mirror and says, "Mirror, Mirror on the wall, who's the fairest of them all?" The teacher can also walk around the room with a mirror approaching different students and asking them what they see when they look at themselves in the mirror. The teacher will display the list of all the lessons learned in the book (see Grades K – 1 on page 62) and use this list to discuss the importance of embracing our uniqueness while always striving to embrace the listed positive behaviors. Roll out Kraft paper and have students trace each other's bodies. Each student will create a representation of themselves using magazines, markers and other craft objects. Each student must incorporate at least 7 of their unique qualities into their depiction.

Notes

DON'T BE THAT KID!™
AT SCHOOL

Resources

DON'T BE THAT KID!

DON'T BE THAT KID! PLEDGE

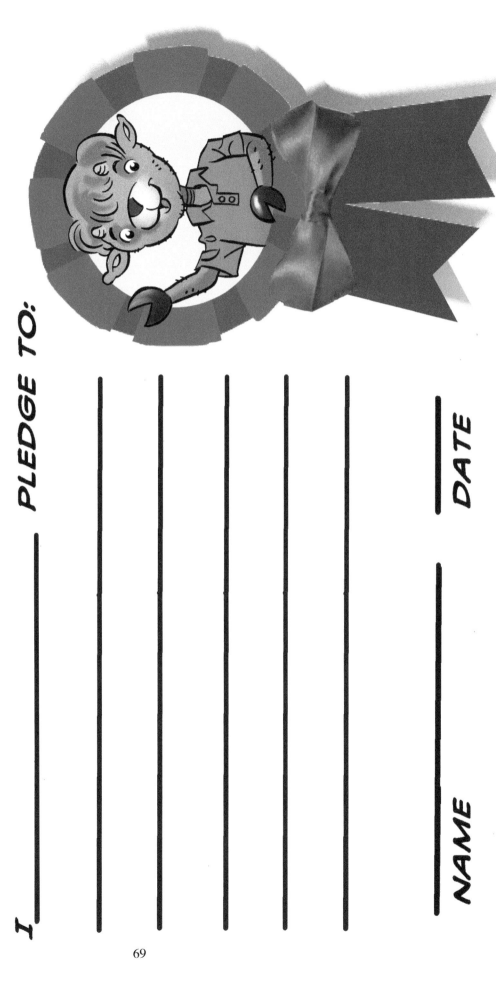

PLEDGE TO:

I _____

_____

_____

_____

_____

_____

_____ _____
NAME   DATE

69

DON'T BE THAT KID!

_____ FAMILY CREST

Lois McGuire
Author

Lois McGuire has 35 years of teaching and leadership experience in the field of education. She began her career as a 4th and 5th grade teacher and retired as the Superintendent of Schools of a highly acclaimed K – 12 school district in New Jersey.

Lois has a strong record of accomplishment in the areas of instructional supervision, curriculum development/direction, personnel issues at all levels, public relations, budgeting, facilities and grant writing. She received many honors as an educator including being awarded seven Best Practices Awards by the New Jersey Department of Education, nine Awards of Excellence from New Jersey School Boards and the New Jersey Coalition of Educational Leaders Award for Outstanding Service and Leadership. She was selected to join New Jersey Governor Thomas Kean at the Governor's Conference in Cincinnati to discuss youth-at-risk. She has been a consultant to the U.S. Department of Education and the N.J. Department of Education on such topics as parent involvement in the schools, career development for children, character education, positive communication skills and strategic planning.

Lois earned her Doctorate in Education from Rutgers University. She was an adjunct professor at Rutgers, Bloomfield College and St. Peter's College where she taught courses in the areas of education, psychology and human relations.

Lois presently lives in Florida with her husband, Jim. She wrote Don't Be That KID! At School and the Don't Be That KID! At School Resource Guide to help educators and parents guide their children through the maze of building essential positive character traits.

Please visit her website at: www.dontbethatkid.net

Jorge Pacheco
Illustrator

Jorge Pacheco has been a professional illustrator for the past 30 years. He has illustrated several children's books including the one you are holding in your hands. Mr.Pacheco has worked for almost every major Comic Book company including Dark Horse Comics, DC Comics, IDW Comics and Archie Comics. Mr. Pacheco was staff artist for Harvey Comics/Entertainment and has drawn many famous licensed characters, such as Casper the friendly Ghost, The Flintstones, Bullwinkle and Rocky, Angry Birds and he even worked briefly for Jim (Garfield) Davis. He also had his own syndicated cartoon strip CEO Dad. Mr. Pacheco has spoken at both the Chuck Jones Center for Creativity & the Charles M. Schulz Museum and Research Center.

CPSIA information can be obtained
at www.ICGtesting.com
Printed in the USA
JSHW022108300919
1686JS00001B/1